DEATH'S DOPPELGÄNGER

IS TRUTH

AHSAHTA PRESS
BOISE, IDAHO
2012

THE NEW SERIES
#50

COUNTERPART

ELIZABETH ROBINSON

Ahsahta Press, Boise State University, Boise, Idaho 83725-1525
ahsahtapress.org
Cover design by Raúl Peña / Quemadura
from a photograph by Jonah Morris
Book design by Janet Holmes
Printed in Canada

LIBRARY OF CONGRESS CATALOGING-IN-PUBLICATION DATA

Robinson, Elizabeth, 1961-
Counterpart / by Elizabeth Robinson.
p. cm. — (The new series ; no. 50)
Poems.
ISBN 978-1-934103-34-0 (PBK. : ALK. PAPER)
ISBN 1-934103-34-9 (PBK. : ALK. PAPER)
I. Title.
PS3568.O2883C68 2012
811'.54—DC23
2012023447

CONTENTS

FOR COLLEEN LOOKINGBILL,
COUNTERPART IN THE BEST OF WAYS

You find it pleasing to plunge into the bosom of your image.

CHARLES BAUDELAIRE

The sense of becoming disturbingly real to yourself, that point where the interior conversations begin, like daylight picking its way over a bridge, over there to the further shore to shine its brightest. The difficult shell halved and the sparse interior looked into, a voice appearing and disappearing with the light that fell on one's single self. Difficult to arrange this monodony. A necessity, the act of discovering where the self starts, hears itself, and repeats the instructions.

BARBARA GUEST

TURN

The one sharp kernel
makes its bitter
seedling.

Seedling
tendered at the end
of the year.

Some light
year

closing,
wrung out

or out
of seed comes
the green aperture,

bitter, tender, self-
pursuing.

Who am I? If this once I were to rely on a proverb, then perhaps everything would amount to knowing whom I "haunt." I must admit that this last word is misleading, tending to establish between certain beings and myself relations that are stranger, more inescapable, more disturbing than I intended. Such a word means much more than it says, makes me, still alive, play a ghostly part, evidently referring to what I must have ceased to be in order to be who I am.

ANDRÉ BRETON

We say it looks familiar but not my face and not looking where one thinks to see it and not in the window passing quickly by.

MARTHA RONK

I, a hand, reached into the sea for a piece of the sea.
What I brought out,

piece of liquid, split my hand in two.
Spilt.

And from the gash came an interpolation
fascinated with its own blood.

O, the tidy world, and how from
this clear rupture comes

a web of great delicacy, clearing away fluid,
detritus, and charting the next

destination of affect.

She had turned around or inside out

and found herself spelt as two.

Sea more paltry than hand.
Implanted in this disappointment

comes a parity not besotted,
only sotted.

This much ocean one could drink down
with a single fist

where it would surely rain
evenly down the two throats

charted clearly in its own sodden web.
Seized and incised.

What I think of as a story is only what I think it is, and
there I am alone in all the world. Pretend it is a slight,
meandering path. And there I go. Here's a fleshy zipper
that opens in my belly, and I unzip and open and then
there I go. Inside and down the path.

Stuck, I am stuck in a small child's possessiveness: mine.
I want my own narrative. I fit the flesh legs over my
own, I wear the blue eyes atop my own vision. I double
back my own tongue to let it taste itself.

But I taste another body's voice.

And so all matter is made of words.
All matter is made of blood which runs through the
ears and tongue so that a body may make words for it.
Interminable and perfect circle. I have said that before;
before that I have said.

In the battle of word and flesh, I am a coward, an
undiscerner.

Let this self pick up its path and carry its own body. Let
it read aloud.

(She reads aloud the text she finds, reads it to the posture of the landscape before her, selves arrayed like a row of trees.)

The trees have fingers, leaves, that silver and clap like cymbals: *chh!*

"In the beginning"

Chh!

"Was the w—"

"And the w— was made —"

"And the"

Chh!

"Was with"

"Flesh"

Chh! Chh!

There the entry caves in, the solitary recruit flees, the
body can channel the path no more. "Mine," is what
the body would have said, had it stayed. But the tongue
comes back to me, calls me deserter, sweetened by
indecision, works the zipper of flesh toward amnesty.

The trees' array of selves shivers, but has no more
capacity for sound or matter.

SANCTUARY

Do you mind, she asked,

if I steal a bit from you. This

she asked again and again until

I discerned that the mere—

the mere asking

got her what she wanted.

Do you mind if I steal

a bit from you, I murmured

to myself, forgetting she stood by.

      Echo like a candle in a cathedral.

      Bit as in bite.

As she repeated and then

repeated herself, I felt the uneven

light, smelled

the warm wax, rising,

as heat does, to the face.

I felt her bite the echo from me,

from the great, arcing rose window face of me,

bought and stolen from

me, irregular

with rising warmth.

She seemed familiar to me though I could not see her face.

Something in the clothes and the bent head made me feel I had often seen her before.

As I drew near the fire the woman stopped stirring the pot and rose to greet me. When we faced each other I felt my heart give a convulsive leap and stop. The woman who stood before me was me.

LEONORA CARRINGTON

THE GOLEM

SLEEP

Unyielding, beneath us,
and yet a morsel to be scavenged,

capitulating against all
other loss.

Against irrelevant loss
what flies away —

a thing one cannot be rid of.

Against its savoring query.

Sleep in its rounded mound,
soft and ashy.
Sleep — feathers of the unformed —
and ample to fill a pillowcase, then
blow from its seams
the indentation of the head that never was.

Again.

A summons
reneged. That drowsing
finger, charcoaled,
smears off the first letter
of any word's repose,

or its soft powder
fills in the impression.

Death's doppelgänger
is truth.

The uncanny, the resolute
inventory of witness,

means a visitor came

hastily

trafficking

one desire for another.

Perfect equilibrium

this is

whose exchange makes flee
the redundant voice

fitted, exquisite

to its intended.

The lost photograph found again,

become a mirror.

One site in the alphabet
needs mending.

What might be provender
releases its dissimilar

twin: empty hourglass
upended.

Corybantic silence,

unravel the echoes stitch
by stitch to make such cloak

then wear it. As in the gait,
uneven, "of a man forever in fear of falling"

so as to see to
the restoration of that letter.

Whose walls are Golem, who

dared mimicry.

Thy face, its archaic language
made immobile with
other language

impaired or contracting.

Beauty is vanity's quackery,
so that the undoing

of the domicile
is its own waxen

distance from animation.

PUNCH

"You've shut us off good and proper from
the outer world. Not one word has got
itself spoken since you shut the window."

What libation
we brew
is history.

And intoxicants
are otherwise
recounted as

the true reflection
of an evasive subject —

this memory into which
one can only be lowered

and impact perilous.

Therefore a toast:

to the image who

was graven, recognized,
recognized, or fallen.

May you resurge.

They are or were
a brigade of hobgoblins, crooks,
paupers

who followed.

And who fed them.

And why

were their spoons
chained to the table, their

bowls ground into
the ruts of the table's surface.

I heard a story once about a man whose arm
caught in the gears of a machine. It was winter
in the north; he was in immediate danger of
freezing. So he hacked his own arm off and
escaped with his life.

Not they, the beggars, those spooks—
but an alternative, the thing
(—disarmed, if you'll excuse the pun—)
embedded in, storylike:

And on page___, it relates
how their benefactor
broke down and wept each year
on the anniversary of his narrative.

AWAKE

Alertness and sorrow
revolve on the same hinge;

just as his hand
sweeps your brow —

the one profile
leaning upon the other —

until all the wisdom
of his hand

becomes as fixed as its caress.

What waking dream
replenishes itself

with time. Skin
laments on skin.

In this, its permission
to enter.

The purpose of the blanket
is not to cover but to fall.

You were made to
recognize, but poorly,

your lover.   A puppet

crudely carved in your likeness

beseeches your help.
Thus your fine seam
suspends the curtain

between. And your reflection bleaches
its own fabric, whose referral
is late and harassed.

Ghosts' intention
is that we learn

not to be appeased
but, differently,
to be patient,
i.e.,

the trap door leads
ultimately

up. Vented star:

the place of absolute
security crouches
there, ready

by supererogation

to scare away any
thorough mortal.

All this pandering
lumen by lumen

to an ache

when the perfect

symmetry of a face
would have sufficed.

Who
harbors this correspondence.

The shadow
falls from

the side of the mouth

directly to the listener's lips.

Distress turns the sheaves of equilibria
back, like hands of a clock.

Time was, these indicating hands
leant into flesh, were the sum of

a breathing body. This dress
clothes time, and for what interval

the body holds up the fabric. What
spare moment opens on this script.

The stress of the syllable in its circularity,
hilarity blanched like the clock face. Concatenated

time brushes over rhyme to reach
her, inept balance, book whose spine

turns, toward an interval of the
recess of the body, lair, this rest:

summons of a body breathing
address. Waning hands due this clock.

FEAR

The new abode, the place I've never been,
circulates through my body,

a goad.

These new friends, my intimates, rupture perfection.
Thus they arrive. Preening.

Loss itself can never supplant fear, prodded

as I am to watch them. Together. How they fornicate

with my selves.

URGE

On your bed,
the dream collects misstatements.

Here the covers are
rumpled, smoothed,
and incrementally
flushed, so

you are implanted
with an urge. A reverie:

      see, the caption clipped from an old photo
      falls into hands
      lent to you
      and mislabeled by miracles.

Iconic, bed-as-book
on which a missive lays.

Your imperfect health
can abide no mystery.

That is,
you borrow something

    where certain removals

placate the dream.

WOMAN

The land before you is perfectly flat,
surely.

Harlot, virgin, catalyst.

Or rather, a bending mirror, a spyglass
that espies the horizon and

makes it delicate with submission.

Why is it so difficult, always, to recognize
a thing for what it is.

The naked is flat, is a syllogism that leads

criss-cross to

a fragile repetition of its own image, called movement.

This all had to do with folds—
the word after word
folded in on itself.

A letter, secreted in the heel
of a shoe, gets ground
into the highway.

It's all creases and secretions
that oil the joints

of a pointing finger

chasing

a bend in the road.
It's the hinge that makes

the cover
close on
a watchface.

TORMENT

The voice recognizes its hoarseness as echo.

Blue glass shimmers in the throat.

On the brow, who will retrace the letters.

Who will fish the relic from my throat.

Who will abandon it there.

What is no longer a throat

humiliates itself, a gullet, a window

rasping in the redundant hands of the giver.

Sentient damage. Bale and chasten, this blue gap.

In the wreck of the world, this instant measures
as unreal: if the unreal can be understood

as translucent. Purified gauge.
Pure material wreckage. That which is allotted.

And what derives from this matter
is innocent of consciousness

so that as one stumbles into its density,
(impediment, organic curve of obstacle,
strange shelter)

the injury one bears away
is residue of innocence: substance

that derives its own light from the impenetrable.

Measure
which has not been shaped by form.

The word seems to have meant the unformed embryo,
that way it cast light,
distended reflection.

Or that the translation meant:
to backtrack.

The word seems to have been a sock
that closed over the footsteps
of a retreating figure.

A shoe led astray, pointing forward,
followed.

Or the translation claimed that what overcame one, literally atop itself,
as incipient shape or movement, would also rescind light.

END

There are scripts, but they are not scripture.

The amnesia was thus perfect at its first attempt:

why would we try to plumb this further?
why does the obdurate watch in envy

as the new truths cave into each other, blissful?

"Have you thought," said Reb Sia to his New Year's guests, "of the importance of the shadow? It is reflection and the sacrifice of reflection. It is man's double and negation."

But do not believe that madness has ever left us. Like pain, it lies in wait for us at each stage, I mean each time we run up against the word hidden in the word, the being buried in the being.

EDMOND JABÈS

DOPPELGÄNGER

Cure the echo.

Identical merges with identity:

one holds in one's body (Twin, Irony, Narcissus),
like its own

trinket, a name repeated.

(Into this world,
the world imports itself. Re-

creation. A sun shining intensely
abolishes all mirrors.

The exact counterpart reconsiders:

two same things mated
with each other abolish

mirrors. The great
heat of acknowledgement

twists, a crease in the cosmos,
fusing this

correspondence.)

Between heaven and hell,
a new cosmology intervenes

and the abolished mirror
generates light.

(Minted on the body
between itself and itself, the tossed coin

turning in mortal air
where all bifurcations of the self
are stamped

Heads or tails,
this meandering planetary coin
absolved from trade, ever.)

Life insists on pursuing this redundancy.

What in the self could imagine a self
conveyed loss surpassing all resemblance.

Arid Narcissus
loves this delusion,

the sound of collision
with the water's surface,

the isolation
of precise sameness

battering itself. Absolute.

How better to translate
than to destroy.

The shape of equivalents
is garbled with wet,
like the synonym for 'evaporate.'

His disabled eye lacks reflection
because reflections lack tears.

Filigree of capillaries
reduced to a pulse. All flesh

blanched by exposure
to its own witness

and stripped
away.

This is you, a mirror caked in clear varnish.

This is you whispering into your own ear.

This is you refusing to hear.

KAZIM ALI

*Watching myself wanting, so far
from my own perception.*

JAMES THOMAS STEVENS

APORIA'S NARRATIVE

I told her I wanted to come see her
and she said, Please.

I said that I was on my way and she
said to come

but that she would not be available for a visit.

The cost

of the travel,

the spare knife in the pocket

that cuts away space

and time. All this she apprehended.

Please,
this word—

the new site to which she has moved,

the ideal.

Hoarse, its address.

MAN FACING SOUTHEAST

after Eliseo Subiela's film

Before you and I were born,
logic defined itself
as the intersection of two planes:
the otherworldly
and this world.

And I met Christ's sister
who revealed to me
her bliss
by the blue fluid
that fell from her mouth.

This,
castle of the rational.
This cell of the sun, you
whose kind decay
opens before me.

Open chastening of the sun
on a bankrupt lawn. You
and your ration, today
encased in sunlight.

Before me, your cell
decays. The open lawn,
the ornate gate heated
in kindness, a logic enfolded.

You
before me, the empty
tin plate, the metallic lawn.
I, whom you loved, and
this

logic of the endless list
is banished from itself.
Like, in kind, to the heat

a cell makes, embedded
in the body. Ornate and
bankrupt. The green lawn.
The frail opening from
ration to rational.

I was given to driving you
in my car
and around my world.
You were given into my care.

Once my car threatened violence
on an innocent one.
But I misremember.

Once when a beggar asked me for money,
you gave him nothing.
And you inquired after my reasoning.
        I do not explain well,
and this rupture resulted
in your disappearance.
Or so I like to remember it.

When we recovered each other,
my conjecture was that two worlds
in violent collision
result in a universe.
But I accepted this idea as one

of only many messages left to me
on my answering machine.

From this vantage
I can choose the pronoun
which designates a self.

       That which is not forgotten
       but which could never
elicit a reply.

Persistent and thematic,
I come forward and through
my body to this ironic and
earnest ode to joy.

The apocalypse
was just a stray cat mewing.
But waking to this quiet annoyance
—the end of the world —
I heard the mortal angel
waiting in my hallway,
her mouth veiled in blue.

Therefore I put
my mouth in hers
to disembowel the kiss.

What other color might
represent haste.

This stick, snapped,
bleeds blue sap.

This awkward dance
before the witnesses.

This night narrows
to the blue steps of the

pattern of the dance.
What torso could

I clutch to mine,
but makes the melody

bulky. I am ridiculous
to make haste eternal.

This is as much a fool
as can hurry. Azure

my sentimental
translation. My other

tongue just says
blue. Snapped in two.

How to disclose what is not seen.
How to please the secret part of the body
that can never be reached from outside.

If two worlds do not collide
or otherwise *do* reverse themselves,
the universe proves itself impossible.

QUEUE

Next in line
he stands.

And behind him
the fugitive from which he came.

He makes
his desire

both ragged and overt.
He embraces the brown twilight.

Some persons say nothing at all.

Open-mouthed, witnesses,

they whimper and they eat.

God administers this soup kitchen,

and he wonders if humility

is a kind of forgetfulness.

Neither does God have a word to say.

We watch this pauper run,

though he could not be said to run

away.

His knapsack falls: temblor, redemption, ultimate
patience.

If you are God,

you can filch food from the kitchen,

but if you are the savior

you follow the orders

of the order.

That order should

entail sequence means

that the savior is always being pursued.

In the end, he is caught

and the audience become witnesses.

Implicated, we can give no judgment

of the performance,

only our ability to watch it.

So it is that with little alteration, the savior

becomes the one saved, that is,

he gives audience to those who

watch, and he hisses.

Forgetful and wordless,

God leans back on the implicate order.

Clarity is, after all,

humble and still

turns around to comfort

the chase that queues up behind it.

> *what fits*　　　　　　　　　*inside a thimble*
> 　　　　　　　　　　　　　　　*a curl*
> *a world*　　　　　　　　　　*Orcus*
> 　　　*was a God*　　　　*of the Dead*
> 　　　　　　　*a three-ring circus*
> 　　　　　　　　　　*an omitted*
> 　　　　　　　　　　　*a double*

ED SMALLFIELD

> *I created myself to death.*

LAURA MORIARTY

Whoever would try to find hell
will only get lost again.

Many resemblances garble their own names.

Pointing fingers are broken off at the stem.

Some antonym, hell-like, elides with hell,
melting on your tongue.

The devil is paternal and tells you to go home.

*

Each has its duty:

a devil resides

in each ear, each nostril,
and bites at the nipples

of the devil.

Each map has its duty.

Each case of mistaken identity.

When one looks at the devils
nesting on the devil, one has

the impression of being caught
in a hall of mirrors.

*

Except not so glossy and reflective
as this body of water.

A pattern shows itself below the surface.

Devil or sea.

The amorous body

of water on which

evil floats, or else

the cast-offs and the wanderers.

All of whom find themselves returning

repeatedly

to the same place, because familiarity

breeds familiarity. And when the devil

says to go home, we, all of us, finally

know where to go.

*

No longer lost, only sluggish,

direction heaves itself like the leviathan

from the bottom of the sea. Minute devils

cling to the plankton it sucks in.

*

This is impossible. The irritant of hell
clings at all orifices.

Heat sashays in through the cold
and offers fake comfort.

The leviathan refuses to stay still.

One is forced to resume one's bitter childhood:
lost, dependent, instilled with duty.

"At last," one wants to say. But the mirror is
eternally and eventually reflective.

Infantile devil, funhouse, ocean-for-drowners,
mismap, obligation, blowhole, itching bites, gloss

and paternity, blue sea of alcohol, toxic resemblance and
synonym, synonym.

DROUGHT

Gray scrolling into blue,
and murky.

Prodigal, the two:
the "us," the "we."

Firmament, solid hand
who caps, suffocates.

The two sole colors.

Hand cupping the dark sun.
Blue smoke. Flow who

extinguishes our commingled dark.
Pinched flame.

DESCENT INTO HELL

homage to Charles Williams

The eye cannot look upon itself,

but can, if arrested or deformed in purpose, look

upon its mate. Vision

makes for spurious relation: how is

a bestiary made, Ouroboros, when

a thing holds another, a part of itself,

inside its own mouth?

The dog chases his hindquarters, just so,

and does he know that when

his tail is clamped in

his teeth, he's become

a serpent, complete

and circular

who

replicates himself?

Yes, an analogy —

The eyes

rest side by side, and having fulfilled

two circuits, transform: now

a pair of lenses. Therefore

two same things achieve different

ends, and no true vision.

Yes,

they are twins. For didn't you, too,

believe in metamorphosis—the way

one creature is always,

always beholden

to another?

Further, the doppelgänger

is the self's midwife. She

stares at her own vagina,

her mouth, the mandorla,

her nether eye, a sleeping body

awakened to this.

A new and circular crucifixion

amid the self-expelling

luminous shade, the residue of

craving repeats itself:

     the sleeper is entitled to

     knowledge of her own existence.

You want pronouns to take on the corporeal,

but they are like the static of a sick-dream,

almost amenable and at the same time,

frizzy, off their marks.

A body is a remembered feature

and not nostalgia

The scent of another body is a molecular fact,

entered the lung

by way of the nostril.

So to be engraved underneath the graffiti of pronoun.

Nostalgia is nocturnal, while pronouns

are constituted of daylight

and the body hovers indecisively at the intersection.

If we try to say "we" as opposed to any singular,

what we allege makes indecision

the decisive site.

This approach is careful not

to express suffering. It says

it wants only to look closely.

After the last breath, it discards

its nose in order to dissect the lung.

Allegation suffocates lament.

Far before this, there was a body

overlapping with a body, perhaps

itself and perhaps not, at which

junctures these divided to bathe
themselves —that was best —

and to go on then to sleep

in their own limited juices,

to sleep odorless in the

itch and prickle of their own

straitened skin.

I would charge myself as pronomial

in this first and singular instance.

Desiccate sadness. The body dissolved

in the dream when the dreamer coughed.

No meaning is found for "cough." There

is no shoulder to look back over or

toward. All is embedded in the lung.

When you say I'll do anything
and you say I'm lying
by you I mean the one looking out at the horizon,
by I I mean a box tethered to the stern of a ship
senseless of its towing

DENNIS PHILLIPS

Someone who'd
been with me

got up with me
and walked in my body

PAT REED

We like singed feathers. Quills. Ink.

We drew our parts with them, two-faced,
apart. Singing or singed,

ink drew

down the body, a dark circle,

hand in hand, a ring
around.

We liked wings,
embedded, their little seeds.
Nacreous heat. Quills
quell

the growth. No flying
allowed, hand in hand

immersed in ink. Nacreous

circle hardening. Ashes,
ahs, eyes fall down.

Icarus, carry us
in your special drowning wings.
We liked them.

Down into a sea of pearly seeds,
black water, dis-
remember, fallen into
oneself, like a sock turned
inside out.

Poxy water. Grained ink,
drawn, quartered, dragged

and re-membered in the
air hand in hand with the air.
Ere. Err. Janus-faced wing.

STUDIES FOR HELL: IV.

Each version gets lost.

They are all astray.

The paternal devil pats

his own back.

What was perfect evaporates,

and the antonym for hell enters

the mouth and melts like a sweet into

resemblance.

Each duty has its own map.

*

Here he is again.

He's a devil

of the devil.

He issues parchment with directions to the treasure.

Bright robbery of direction.

One sees the brightness, but not

controlled as in past iterations.

A precisely broken mirror reflects its own cracks.

*

This intercourse reflects, and

is not so glossy as the sea on which all must float.

Conceive. Hell of water inserted into no water.

They float away, cast offs and wanderers.

      In an insoluble current, they come back.

They come back. The iteration moves

desperately quickly to keep up.

*

Sluggish now, the sense that one

is free rises, a leviathan from the

floor of the sea.

Purported sea floor,

our bluish and dilute devil has now been stolen.

Tell me which synonym

was most valuable, and I can tell you where on the map

it was buried.

*

It's not possible, this hurrying to keep up with loss.

Finding provision detached from its own evil. This bitter
return to childhood and dependence and the inconstant world.

Anonymity, sunken treasure, blowhards, itchy bites, boozy sea,

funhouse, debt, poisonous tether of synonym to resemblance. The
coating that shines from all things, real or imagined.

eat names.

release replica.

CRAIG WATSON

SECRET EDEN

This is the apple

by whom you will know your own tongue:

grown through the vein of the leaf

and pressed away from fruit.

Speak, tongue, with your obedient quiet. Divide,

but do not be divisive.

Now say blessing on the stem, the seed,
the orders of reproduction,

flanked on all sides by
destination.

Pronounce pulp and juice. How they divide from each other
as a fork in the road.

ACKNOWLEDGMENTS

The author thanks the following publications in which poems from this manuscript originally appeared: *Absomaly, Cold Drill, Colorado Review, Conjunctions, Denver Quarterly, Effing Magazine, Illiterate Magazine, Literary Salt, Mary, New American Writing, The New Review, Superflux*.

Very warm thanks also to Nancy Kuhl and Richard Deming for publishing a chapbook, *The Golem*, through Phylum Press.

Ongoing gratitude for friendship, insight, support to Susanne Dyckman, Craig Watson, Brian Teare, and Rusty Morrison and Ken Keegan.

ABOUT THE AUTHOR

ELIZABETH ROBINSON is the author of several collections of poetry including *Pure Descent*, winner of the National Poetry Series, and *Apprehend*, winner of the Fence Modern Poets Prize. Robinson has also received grants from the Fund for Poetry, the Foundation for Contemporary Arts, and the Boomerang Foundation. Educated at Bard College, Brown University, and the Pacific School of Religion, Robinson has most recently served as the Hugo Fellow at the University of Montana.

AHSAHTA PRESS

SAWTOOTH POETRY PRIZE SERIES

2002: Aaron McCollough, *Welkin* (Brenda Hillman, judge)

2003: Graham Foust, *Leave the Room to Itself* (Joe Wenderoth, judge)

2004: Noah Eli Gordon, *The Area of Sound Called the Subtone* (Claudia Rankine, judge)

2005: Karla Kelsey, *Knowledge, Forms, The Aviary* (Carolyn Forché, judge)

2006: Paige Ackerson-Kiely, *In No One's Land* (D. A. Powell, judge)

2007: Rusty Morrison, *the true keeps calm biding its story* (Peter Gizzi, judge)

2008: Barbara Maloutas, *the whole Marie* (C. D. Wright, judge)

2009: Julie Carr, *100 Notes on Violence* (Rae Armantrout, judge)

2010: James Meetze, *Dayglo* (Terrance Hayes, judge)

2011: Karen Rigby, *Chinoiserie* (Paul Hoover, judge)

AHSAHTA PRESS

NEW SERIES

This book is set in Apollo MT type
with Titling Gothic FB Condensed titles
by Ahsahta Press at Boise State University.
Cover design by Raúl Peña / Quemadura
from a photograph by Jonah Morris.
Book design by Janet Holmes.
Printed in Canada.

AHSAHTA PRESS

2012

JANET HOLMES, DIRECTOR

CHRISTOPHER CARUSO

JODI CHILSON

KYLE CRAWFORD

CHARLES GABEL

JESSICA HAMBLETON, *intern*

RYAN HOLMAN

MELISSA HUGHES, *intern*

TORIN JENSEN

ANNIE KNOWLES

STEPHA PETERS

JULIE STRAND